Be an ASTRONOMER

BY NICOLE SHEA

Gareth Stevens
PUBLISHING

Please visit our website, www.garethstevens.com. For a free color catalog of all our high-quality books, call toll free 1-800-542-2595 or fax 1-877-542-2596.

Library of Congress Cataloging-in-Publication Data

Shea, Nicole.
Be an astronomer / by Nicole Shea.
    p. cm. — (Be a scientist!)
Includes index.
ISBN 978-1-4824-1208-6 (pbk.)
ISBN 978-1-4824-1199-7 (6-pack)
ISBN 978-1-4824-1444-8 (library binding)
1. Astronomy — Vocational guidance — Juvenile literature. 2. Astronomy — Juvenile literature. I. Shea, Nicole, 1976-. II. Title.
QB51.5 S47 2015
520—d23

First Edition

Published in 2015 by
Gareth Stevens Publishing
111 East 14th Street, Suite 349
New York, NY 10003

Designer: Katelyn E. Reynolds
Editor: Therese Shea

Photo credits: Cover, p. 1 John Davis/Stocktrek Images/Getty Images; cover, pp. 1–32 (background texture) leungchopan/Shutterstock.com; p. 5 Valerio Pardi/Shutterstock.com; p. 7 NASA, ESA, N. Evans (Harvard-Smithsonian CfA), and H. Bond (STScI); p. 8 Photos.com/Thinkstock.com; pp. 9, 17 NASA; p. 10 The Power of Forever Photography/E+/Getty Images; p. 11 Comstock/Stockbyte/Thinkstock.com; p. 13 NASA/Kepler Mission/Wendy Stenzel; p. 14 Vladimir Arndt/iStock/Thinkstock.com; p. 15 Elenarts/Shutterstock.com; p. 19 NASA, ESA, and M. Livio and the Hubble 20th Anniversary Team (STScI); p. 21 ajbarr/iStock/Thinkstock.com; p. 23 NASA, ESA, and A. Feild (STScI); p. 25 NASA/Dana Berry, SkyWorks Digital; p. 27 Greg Dale/National Geographic/Getty Images; p. 29 Barry Winiker/Photolibrary/Getty Images.

Printed in the United States of America

CPSIA compliance information: Batch #CS15GS: For further information contact Gareth Stevens, New York, New York at 1-800-542-2595.

CONTENTS

Words in the glossary appear in **bold** type
the first time they are used in the text.

WHAT IS AN ASTRONOMER?

Astronomers are scientists who study the universe and the many fascinating objects in it, including the sun, other stars, planets, and moons. They're sometimes called astrophysicists. Some astronomers even study whether faraway planets can support life, so that, like in the movies, people might live somewhere other than Earth someday. Astronomers have one of the most exciting science careers today.

To begin to learn about astronomy, you don't need to sign up for a class or buy special **equipment**. All you need are your eyes and a clear, starry night. A good telescope doesn't hurt, either! Then, find a comfortable chair, lean back, and look up.

WANTED: CURIOSITY AND IMAGINATION

Today's astronomers need curiosity. They need to wonder why a star seems to move in the sky in a certain way or why a moon has a certain shape. Since we can't go to other worlds yet, scientists combine serious research and a bit of imagination to figure out answers to these questions.

There's much, much more in the universe than you can see in the night sky.

EARLY STARGAZERS

For thousands of years, people have looked up at the night sky. Some saw patterns that reminded them of animals or characters from stories. A pattern of stars that has been named is called a constellation. Constellations are helpful for finding certain stars. For example, Polaris, also called the North Star, is located in the constellation Ursa Minor.

As stargazers studied how stars moved, they discovered that Polaris seems to be fixed in the night sky. Travelers could walk toward Polaris and always be sure they were headed north. People began to use other stars to navigate as well as keep track of time.

WHAT IS AN ASTROLOGER?

You might wonder what the difference is between an astrologer and an astronomer. Astrologers study the positions of the sun, moon, and other **celestial** bodies as astronomers do. However, astrologers believe that they have an effect on people's lives and study them to learn what the effect will be. Astrology is an ancient practice in many countries.

Polaris

Ursa Minor

Ursa Major

7

FROM GALILEO TO TODAY

In 1610, an Italian scientist named Galileo looked through a new tool for stargazing, the telescope. He saw four small bright "stars" moving near Jupiter. He watched their movements over several nights and learned that these objects were really moons that were circling, or orbiting, Jupiter.

OBSERVATORIES

Astronomers put the best telescopes on Earth in special buildings called observatories. But since light from space can have trouble traveling through Earth's atmosphere, some observatories are crafts **launched** beyond the atmosphere and into space! The Herschel Space Observatory, for example, helped astronomers discover a step in the process of star formation.

Galileo is often called the "Father of Modern Astronomy."

Above Earth's atmosphere, the Hubble Space Telescope can take incredible pictures and gather a lot of useful information.

Galileo used **optical** telescopes as many astronomers do today. However, these aren't helpful during the day or on cloudy nights. Other telescopes, such as radio telescopes and X-ray telescopes, can be used in daytime and in bad weather. They use waves of energy—radio waves and X-rays—to create images of space objects.

Today's professional astronomers
don't have to look through telescope lenses each
night as Galileo did. They use telescopes that have
cameras attached to them. They can review the images
captured at any time. They also use computers to
gather **data**. In fact, much of an astronomer's day is
spent in an office using computer programs, trying to
figure out what data mean. They also meet with fellow
scientists about their results and write papers that tell
others of their research.

Astronomy is one of the few sciences in which scientists cannot perform experiments directly.
They have to make many observations, sometimes over many years, to test out their ideas.

moon

Venus

Not all bright objects in the sky are stars. Some are planets!

Because the universe is so huge, astronomers usually focus their research on certain areas of astronomy, such as planets, the sun and other stars, or the formation of **galaxies**.

STAR LIGHT, STAR BRIGHT

Finding the planet Venus is easy, even without a telescope. Called both the "Morning Star" and the "Evening Star," it's often the first point of light you see when it starts getting dark. Venus is close to the sun, so reflected sunlight can make it look like the brightest object in the evening sky.

11

PLANETARY ASTRONOMERS

Planetary astronomers study planets, especially how they form, how they move, and what their surface, center, and atmosphere are like. You probably know quite a bit about the eight planets in our **solar system** already. Mercury, Venus, Earth, and Mars are rocky planets. Jupiter, Saturn, Uranus, and Neptune are gas planets. Thanks to astronomers, we know that other planets have seasons and even storms, just like Earth.

Planetary astronomers also study planets beyond our solar system, called exoplanets. They've already found exoplanets orbiting faraway stars with the help of the Kepler space observatory. They hope one day to find a planet with life.

GALAXIES

Our solar system is located in the Milky Way galaxy. There are about 200 billion other stars in our galaxy. Some galaxies are even larger, with more than 100 trillion stars. Astronomers think there may be more than 100 billion galaxies in the universe! That means there are a lot of stars and possible Earthlike planets out there.

The Kepler observatory's mission is to find Earthlike planets. So far, it's found more than 3,500 possible planets. Astronomers have used data sent back from the observatory to **confirm** 167 of these are actual planets.

13

Ever since Galileo looked through his telescope, astronomers have been interested in moons. Planetary astronomers study moons, too. Our moon, like all moons, is a satellite, which is a small object in orbit around a larger one. Astronomers know there's no life on our moon, but they look for life on other moons.

For life as we know it to exist, there needs to be water. Titan, one of Saturn's 62 moons, has many lakes. However, they contain liquid methane and ethane, not water. Still, astronomers say Titan is one of the most Earthlike places in the solar system.

SATURN'S RINGS

Astronomers study the famous rings of Saturn, first seen by Galileo, to find out how satellites act in orbit around a planet. The rings are made of dust, rocks, and ice pulled from Saturn's moons and passing objects such as **comets**. Each ring orbits the planet at a different speed!

The moon is the only place in our solar system, other than Earth, that people have actually visited.

The Cassini-Huygens spacecraft has given us a great view of Saturn and its moons.

15

STELLAR ASTRONOMY

Some astronomers focus on the study of stars, or stellar astronomy. They research how stars are born, change, and finally die. Our sun is like other stars in that it's a ball of gas that changes hydrogen into helium in a process called nuclear fusion. By comparing our sun to many other stars, astronomers have discovered that our sun is a medium-sized star. Some stars, like red giants, are so big that a few thousand of our sun could fit inside!

Astronomers have learned that many solar systems have pairs of stars, called binary stars. Planets can orbit binary stars, too.

SUNSHINE TIMES TWO

Although we may see stars as single points of light, astronomers believe that most of the stars we see are actually two stars! They're so far away that they look like single dots. In 1802, William Herschel first used the word "binary" for these double stars. He found about 700 pairs of stars during his lifetime.

smallest Kepler
red giant

our sun

largest Kepler red giant

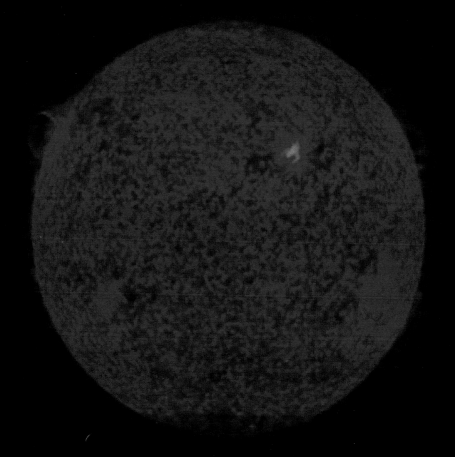

17

One of the most interesting things stellar astronomers look for is a huge **explosion** called a supernova. A supernova occurs when a large star **collapses**. Because the explosion can shine brighter than an entire galaxy, supernovas help astronomers find galaxies they haven't discovered before.

Astronomers can also use supernovas to measure distances in space. They know how bright a supernova usually is for certain types of exploding stars. However, the farther away a supernova is, the dimmer it appears to be. Astronomers use the brightness of the supernova to figure out its distance. Objects like supernovas used to find distances in space are called standard candles.

THE SOUNDS OF SUPERNOVAS

Astronomers are finding out new information about supernovas all the time. For example, they now know that supernovas make a kind of humming noise before exploding. You might think that supernovas don't happen that often, but astronomers believe that one occurs about every second in the universe!

The matter given off by a supernova may come together to form new stars and planets.

19

MEASURING SPACE

When astronomers record an object's distance, they use a unit of measurement called a light-year. A light-year is the distance light travels in 1 year, which is about 5.88 trillion miles (9.5 trillion km). The farther away something is, the longer it takes for light to travel to us. So, when astronomers see the light from a star 4 light-years away, they're seeing what it looked like 4 years ago.

The distance from our sun to the nearest star is about 4.24 light-years. The nearest galaxy is about 25,000 light-years from our solar system. That means that the stars astronomers are looking at appear as they were 25,000 years ago!

EVERYTHING IN MOTION

Many scientists believe that the universe is expanding. Imagine space is like a black rubber sheet with little motorized cars as the stars. Now, imagine stretching the rubber sheet. Not only do the cars (or stars) move, but the space they're traveling on is moving, too!

The Andromeda galaxy is the closest spiral galaxy to us. A spiral galaxy is one that circles out from a point. Our Milky Way galaxy is a spiral galaxy, too.

METEORS, COMETS, AND ASTEROIDS

Besides stars, moons, and planets, astronomers watch for other objects that sometimes come much closer to Earth than we'd like. Have you ever seen a "shooting star"? Shooting stars aren't stars but meteors, which are small burning pieces of rock traveling through Earth's atmosphere. If they manage to reach the ground, they're called meteorites.

Comets are large pieces of rock, ice, and other matter. As they near the sun, the ice melts and releases dust, creating a "tail." Some comets are periodic visitors to Earth's skies, passing by regularly after a certain number of years.

Asteroids are made of rock and sometimes metal, mostly nickel and iron. They can be small or very large.

KEEPING AN EYE ON THE SKY

All the work that **amateur** and professional astronomers do keeping an eye on meteors, comets, and asteroids is important. Every so often, one of these hits the ground with great force. In fact, scientists think that an asteroid may have crashed to Earth 65 million years ago, wiping out the dinosaurs.

FAMOUS COMETS

NAME	FAMOUS FOR	DISCOVERED
Halley	appearing about every 76 years	1705
Shoemaker-Levy 9	crashing into Jupiter	1993
Hale-Bopp	stayed visible for 18 months	1995
Hyakutake	one of the longest tails seen	1996
McNaught (C/2006 P1)	fan-shaped tail; very bright	2007

The name "comet" comes from a Greek word meaning "hair of the head." People thought the tail looked like long hair. Comets can have more than one tail. This one has six!

BLACK HOLE DETECTIVES

Sometimes, astronomers have to be detectives, looking for something no one can see. Black holes form from dying stars. Their mass may collapse until their **gravity** is so strong that nothing, not even light, can escape.

Since there's no light coming from black holes, they're impossible to see. However, astronomers can tell that a black hole is there by tracking its effects on nearby stars and planets. For example, nearby matter releases X-rays.

There's a huge black hole at the center of our Milky Way galaxy. It's more than 4 million times more massive than our sun!

EVENT HORIZON TELESCOPE

Astronomers and other scientists created a special telescope in 2013 that they hope will capture the first image of a black hole's event horizon. The event horizon is the point around a black hole where it becomes impossible for anything to escape its gravity.

STUDENTS OF THE STARS

If the information in this book is interesting to you, you should consider a career in astronomy. There aren't many professional astronomers, just a few thousand in the United States. They spend many years in school learning as much as they can about the universe. In college, they take classes such as **physics**, math, and, of course, astronomy. After college, they go on to earn master's and doctoral degrees.

Many astronomers become teachers and professors. Others work at NASA (National Aeronautics and Space Administration) or at a ground observatory, such as Kitt Peak National Observatory in Arizona and Cerro Tololo Interamerican Observatory in the country of Chile.

THE ASP

There are organizations for both amateur and professional astronomers. One is called the Astronomical Society of the Pacific (ASP), and it's for anyone interested in astronomy. The ASP is the largest general astronomy society in the world, with members from more than 70 countries.

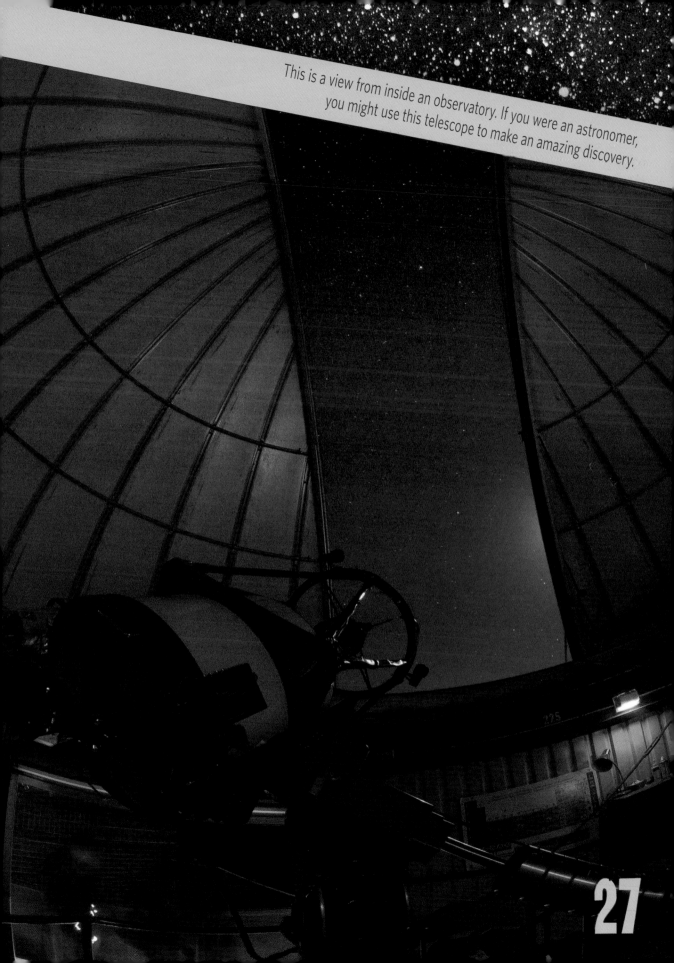

This is a view from inside an observatory. If you were an astronomer, you might use this telescope to make an amazing discovery.

You can start your astronomy studies right now. First, read all you can about astronomy at your school and local library. Scientists are making new discoveries every day, so check NASA's website as often as you can to find the most up-to-date information. Visit observatories and planetariums so you can benefit from the latest astronomy equipment. In school, classes in math, science, and computers are all important to astronomy. Astronomers also need to be good researchers and writers.

Talk to other people interested in the universe. You could even start an astronomy club. Most of all, keep stargazing. You never know what you'll see!

PLANETARIUMS

A planetarium is a place where you can see what the night sky looks like, no matter the time of day. It has a large room with a curved ceiling and many seats. A special machine shines images on the ceiling and shows the stars and other objects in the night sky. Many planetariums also have telescopes.

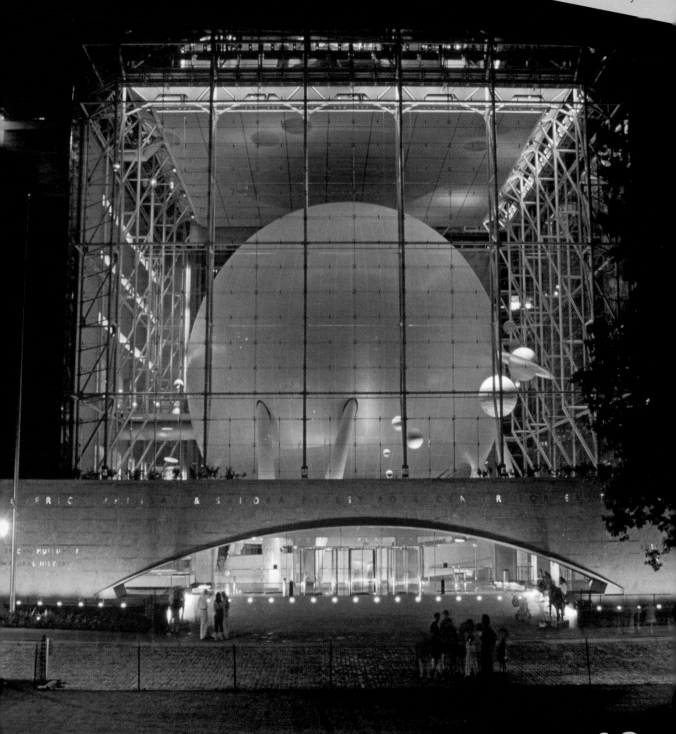

This is the planetarium at the American Museum of Natural History in New York City.

29

GLOSSARY

amateur: someone who does something without pay

celestial: having to do with something in the sky or space

collapse: to fall down or cave in

comet: a space object made of ice and dust that has a long glowing tail when it passes close to the sun

confirm: to find to be true

data: facts and figures

equipment: tools, clothing, and other items needed for a job

explosion: a sudden release of energy

galaxy: a large group of stars, planets, gas, and dust that form a unit within the universe

gravity: the force that pulls objects toward the center of a planet or star

launch: to send out with great force

optical: having to do with the sense of sight

physics: the study of matter, energy, force, and motion, and the relationship among them

solar system: the sun and all the space objects that orbit it, including the planets and their moons

FOR MORE INFORMATION

BOOKS

Consolmagno, Guy, and Dan M. Davis. *Turn Left at Orion: Hundreds of Night Sky Objects to See in a Home Telescope—and How to Find Them.* New York, NY: Cambridge University Press, 2011.

Dinwiddie, Robert, et. al. *Stars and Planets.* New York, NY: DK Publishing, 2012.

Hughes, Catherine. *First Big Book of Space.* Washington, DC: National Geographic, 2012.

WEBSITES

Astronomy for Kids
www.frontiernet.net/~kidpower/astronomy.html
Read more about the celestial objects in our universe, and check out incredible photos from the Hubble Space Telescope.

Cosmos for Kids
www.cosmos4kids.com
This site has great information on our solar system and galaxy.

Star Child
starchild.gsfc.nasa.gov/docs/StarChild/StarChild.html
Check out NASA's "learning center for young astronomers."

INDEX